How to
Do and Say
in England

How to
Do and Say
in England

A trim kompaktikum for Students of Englisch talk
and society behaviourism

Anthony Robertson

Illustrated by J. S. Goodall

PRION

This edition published in 2001 by
Prion Books Limited
Imperial Works,Perren Street,
London NW5 3ED
www.prionbooks.com

First published in 1936

ISBN 1-85375-455-2

Jacket design by gray 318

Printed and bound in Great Britain by
Creative Print & Design Ltd., Ebbw Vale

Contents

Englisch Introduction   ix
1. Society   1
2. Sport   15
3. Lov   39
4. Humoristics   49
5. Approval of Animals   57
6. London   69
7. Countriside   85
8. Anniversaries   99
   Two Epistles for Idiomatik Study   111

Appreciative

"Since pouring over How to Do and Say in England, my Englisch is developed beyond recognition!"— ALBRECHT LAMPRECHT RUPRECHT BIERSÄUFER (*Rechtslehrer*, Trinkenstein-am-Wein).

Englisch Introduction

STUDENTS!

I am anxious to ensure you that in this little bookling, you shall find the most idiomatik Englisch that money can buy. It is of course for slightly forward students who already have a notion or two of the tonguework and vokabular and for those who intend that they themselves and the Best People shall be an intermixture. In the words of my good old chum (*Kamerad*), Dr. Curtius Bohl, '*Die Highlife und Bestcircles—die sind die Hauptsachen.*'

For my part, I go into society any amount without blunder; not I he who should instruct you to do or say the wrong thing, by Jove! not a bit! I am he who has scampered in person with the foxcatchers, supped in the Best drawingrooms and conferred with Society. I know all the celebriates!

In this bookling you shall discover true blue englisch conversationalism, specimen epistles and hints on deporting yourself, all written in lovely language, which should be aped. For my part, would I be surprised if even englisch students helped themselves to my teachings as a guide to correctitude? Oh no! I can't see myself being!

1.

Society

Society

STUDENTS!

The idea is that you are penetrating a drawing-room in a social way. This is the Right Thing:

(1) If you are a gent., you are at once to raise your bowler cap to the hostess with a nice grin and say 'Dear Milady Suchandso, how do you do, eh?' or 'How are you being, really?'

[Pronunciation: *Hau du ju du, e? Hau ar ju bi'ing, ri'äli?*]

(2) If you are a milady, you say the samething, also, but do not touch the hat. Leave it up there.

Then all shake themselves by the hand.

When it has been sat down, you may commence the chattering by drawing attention to the weather or to sports.

Do not dispute in a political way, for this is undone in drawingrooms. It is bad mannerisms.

It is quite the Right Thing to give vent to an observation of this nature: 'This rain is not at all to my taste, you know. It is a bit thick, eh? Oh so disgruntling!'

[*Dhis rehn is nöt at al tu mei tehst, ju noh. It is a bitt dhik, e? O so disgröntling!*]

Before it has been sat down, the bowler cap must

be placed in the hands of a servingman together with the glofes and the cane or umbrello.

Sit uprighteously—do not lounche about as if you were ever such a lackadaisi.

Do not cough, sneese or contract the hicquet, which might offend.

If you are offered a nice cup of tea, do not be faddi. You must aver that you relish it equivocalli well whether together with or together without sugre, milck or citron. As for dainties, be sure to choose out such that you can neatly devour without noisiness or clumsy carrying-on.

On taking a departure:

(1) If you are a gent., bow deeply to the hostess and, if you know her closely, salute her hand. (First sweep away all trace of confection or sweetmeat from the beard.)

(2) A lady should grin slightly and lend a hand by way of saying 'Goodbi!'

You must say: 'I thank. I am so pleased, I have had a so roaring good-time!'
[*Ei dhank. Ei äm so pliesd, ei häw hädd ä so rorring gudd teim!*]

For smoking gentry:

If you care for lighting up after consumption of tea, recall all this: (1) It is not the Right Thing to ignight pipes in a drawingroom, lest the ladies get a whiff of it.

(2) Await persuasion by the hostess.

(3) If you proffer your own weeds, remember that all must have a chance at them and do not pass about a half empty container.

(4) Do not asch the rug.

(5) The correct cigarettes in England are un-corked.

Conversation Piece

LORD SMITH. I am going into society. Are you also
  invited as well?

VISCOUNT BROWN. Always I am invited.

[*They go into society.*

LORD SMITH. Let us commence a conversation with
  these lords.

VISCOUNT BROWN. Consider what you are about! One
  would think you a not a gentleman. Dear me! You
  have to be introduced by the lady of the house.

LORD ROBINSON. There are beautiful ladies here, splendid toilets.

LORD SMITH. It is hot. The air is so thick, one can hardly see eachother.

VISCOUNT BROWN. Take some sherbert, some limonade?

LORD ROBINSON. Thanks—I can be without it.

LORD SMITH. I perceive champagne wine, bubbli.

LORD ROBINSON. Let us all swallow the bubbli!

[*All swallow.*

ALL. Ah ! the topping englisch society!

VISCOUNT BROWN. We are in the Bestcircles! How comfortable !

THE LADY OF THE HOUSE. Shall I present you to many nobles?

LORD SMITH. O do! First, to yonder classi old gentleman!

LADY OF THE HOUSE. He there is my butler!

LORD SMITH (*hastefully*). I was but in fun!

[*The others have a laugh up their sleeve.*

Evening-eat.
How to deport yourself at a meal.

STUDENTS!

The evening-eat, you shall know, is styled Dinner and is of serious import, for it is not only a chance to tuck-in, but is always used also as an occasion for being well-bred and showing what first-class society you are. So pay me some attention, I do insist!

After the aperitiv, at which one need but chitter-chatter and need not say weighty things, each gentleman is supplied with one of the ladies to show her the way to the repast, arm in arm, as pleasant as you please—a good old englisch custom which prevents congestion at the entrance to the meal-room. A sedate step is correct. Never show too much eagerness and drag her along, for one must pretend to forget about the repast.

At table conversation may be heavier and a general topik may be discussed quiescently—do not be controversial, which is unsuitable to table.

Remember: Do not say things with the mouth stuffed with fare.

Do not provide your plate before plying others with each disch.

He who consumes peas by the knifeful is the laughing-stick of those present. Therefor never do this in all seriousness. It is better to forego a pea than to muster as one of the not the Best People.

Opine kindly on what is served up as eatables. Say: 'Yes, yes, very nice of course. Some flavour!'

[*Jess, jess, weri neiss, ow corss. Söm flehwör!*]

Eschew the food without clamour, lest you be called 'Oh what a grunter! Porki!'

[*O! huott ä grönter! Porki!*]

Never show a preference for overmuch alcoholiks, for those present are sure to pass remarques subsequently.

Do not elbow the table or lean across. Such is not satisfactory form.

If you make a mistake of behaviourism, cover it over by pretending that you had been intending to be laughable and that really of course you were in the know and could carry on correctly if you tried.

In fact from beginning to end, act with restraint and on no account let on that you are enchoying the grubb.

If you take a rosy view of some pretti girl next alongside, do not nudge or tikle, but merely smile gravely and aver 'We seem to be getting on like a cat on hot bricks, eh? You charm me, oh really!'

[*Ui sihm tu bi getting ön leik ä cätt ön hött brikss, e? Ju tscharm mi, o riä'li!*]

Conversation Piece

This piece is typical of an only by men being consumed dinner, a stag-party. At a stag-party, you can go the whole hog.

LORD SMITH. (*The host.*) The gong has banged. Let us set to!

VISCOUNT BROWN. First let us grace.

[*They grace*

LORD SMITH. Do not sup your broth so. It is not-done. It is putrid bad form!

LORD ROBINSON. It is putrid bad broth!

LORD SMITH. What? Eh, I say! But no, I see what! You are pulling me by the legs,* eh? Well, I am not one of those fellows who grumple when they are being pulled by the legs. I can laugh it off at myself! * ever so merrily.

[*Laughs at himself.*

*Englisch custom.

10

VISCOUNT BROWN. What a fisch! Scrumptious! I smack my lip* with love for this tasty disch of fresch, fried fisch. I beg, pass please the saltbox.

LORD SMITH. There is now chops and juggled hare.

       [All lick their chops.*

LORD SMITH. Pray, the chops, I hope, are not over-done?

LORD ROBINSON. Nay, this one is quite undone, I assure you.

VISCOUNT BROWN. Shall I dine wisely or twice as well?

LORD ROBINSON. It is the same thing. Aha! How I am a funny choker! Ho! Ho! It is good to make chokes, while at meat, as a digestive.

       [All choke together.

LORD SMITH. What fun!

VISCOUNT BROWN. Quite first-hole!

LORD ROBINSON. Yum! Yum!

LORD SMITH. May I help you with the gravy?

LORD ROBINSON. Thanks no. There is already a sufficiency in my spoon.

LORD SMITH. Pray chew some slices of this sweetie. It is Rolly-Polo.

VISCOUNT BROWN. Nay, I always pass the pudding by. It distresses my within.

LORD SMITH. Then sample this desert fruit or pastry cake.

VISCOUNT BROWN. Thanks I shall take the cake.*

LORD SMITH. Here is porto and cigars. Let us drink ourselves under the table.*

VISCOUNT BROWN.(*under the table, ho! ho!*). How my good wife, who remains at home, shall skold yours truly! Some reprimandum for my part, O!

ALL. Ho! Ho!

*Englisch custom.

Picknik or Roughing Along Somehow

STUDENTS!

If you go upon an expedition with the idea of eating and drinking in the openair, there are one or two points you must be apprehensive about. Behaviourism may be looser, but yet there are social laws of which you must sit up and take notice about, even beyond doors.

(1) Dress. If a gent., you may go about wearing no tie at all and still muster as one who is a perfect gentleperson, while white flanneaux give a sporti tinge to the appearance. Klub blazer every time.

If of the softer sex, you are permitted to say 'Goodbi!' to your hosen and a light white frocque is mentionable, if of the best stuff that money can buy.

(2) How to carry-on. Be of assistance. It is usually a question of all hands to the plough and no heeltapps. For the menpeople, there will be undoing of tin-canns and the stiffer tasks, while for the ladifolk much work such as handing over the good things and outpouring of the liquid assets, when they have been de-stoppered by the he-men of the parti.

To schirk is to show that you are not a chip of the old salt and have not the well-known old englisch gutz. It is always correct to have these.

(3) Countenance. Always be cheeri and not the

De-stoppered by the he-man of the parti

moist blanket, which englisch folk do not like you to go in for being. If you are cooking the edibilities over a driftwood fire and the ignition should collapse, making it necessary to attempt further combustion with the ultimate lucifer, do not pull some long faces, but give a merry 'Ho! Ho!' and pass a glad remarque. For instance—'Gracious! Oh, what a pretti to-do! But never mind, I say, try, try some more, eh? Better late than not at all.'

(*Greh'schöss! O, huott ä pritti tu–du! Bött näwär meindd, ei seh, trei, trei söm mor, e? Bätter leht dhann nött ätt öll?*)

Never cast a cigarette end into an ambusch, lest blaze develop.

Never relinquisch ods and ends. To permit rubbisch to repose on the turf is not even the privilege of the best people.

2.

Sport

Sport

You may be excused from playing cricket and foutbal and still rank nice and high, but you must watch such sport and talk of it. In any case must you do something and be proficient if humanely possible.

Sport Chat

LORD SMITH. Let us telefone some of the Best People and propose a party at cricket, foutbal, tennice, rogger, sogger, pingping, horse-polo or le croquet.

LORD ROBINSON. I pooh-pooh the idea. It rains cat and dog, with thunder. Besides, my hat, there is snow, I hear. Too bad!

VISCOUNT BROWN. I too pooh-pooh the idea. Let us therefor commence a conversation of a sporty species, eh what?

LORD SMITH. Are we all sporty public schoolers?

LORD ROBINSON and VISCOUNT BROWN. Indeed, of course we naturally attended the very Best establishment. Every day.

LORD SMITH. Not only gained I a position in the first fifdeen, but also one at the same time, in the second!

VISCOUNT BROWN. I played the part of the man who defends the sticks. The goalbird.

LORD ROBINSON. Pay attention lo! It schines. Let us go a-schooting.

[They go and a-schoot

A-Schooting

LORD SMITH. Halloo! Whoopee! Oskar the dog has found something; he stands. Peace! It is a partridge!

VISCOUNT BROWN. I perceive many braces.

LORD ROBINSON. Let us enter the spot where they have perched.

That is enough sport for to-day

LORD SMITH. Alas! My birdshot passed the partridge by and entered the beater while he bended. Dear! Dear!

VISCOUNT BROWN. He squeals.

LORD ROBINSON. That is enough sport for to-day. Let us carry him into the house.

A SERVINGMAN. Milords, the lunchion awaits.

THE SPORTY LORDS. We will at once munch the lunch. Let us bang off our guns before entering.

THE SERVINGMAN. How sporty are the milords!

THE BEATER. Would that I had not bended!

A-Golfing

Although a-golfing is not dangerous, it is popular in England and a trim style is admired. Remain alert to dissuade yourself from behaving against the regulations. The code of behaviourism is very tight.

Conversation Piece

LORD SMITH. Now I have to do this hole in boger to vainquisch, and should I be he who loses two more holes, I shall have to treat refreschments.

VISCOUNT BROWN. Let me, I pray, instruct you which things to observe. Eye the ball without stint and when at ease, swing for it.

LORD ROBINSON. It is not all done by talk. What next! Those who sport behind us gather impatience. Listen!

A BEHIND THEM COMING GENTLEMAN. Hi there! I say! Do not think, I beg, that we are fond of standing about for many days! Swing, I pray, and permit us to proceed!

LORD SMITH. Who are these who address us in a fashion so perempt?

VISCOUNT BROWN. I think it is a mixed fearsome.

LORD SMITH. Then perchance I should stroke the ball lest they should catch us up and behave as if they were in not a good temper. Where is my maschi?

[He plays on to a lawn.

Some gasch in the prettie!

21

VISCOUNT BROWN. Bravo! But oh my! Some gasch you have cut in the prettie! Of course the slice must be restored, but I see it nowhere to be found.

LORD SMITH. Come along, do! What a fuss about you make! I will dispatch one of the cabbies. He shall make all safe and sound some more. Anyway my ball lies on the lawn!

LORD ROBINSON. But it is the wrong lawn. Ho! Ho!

LORD SMITH. Ei! Tch! Too bad! Never mind I will resume my maschi and try again.

THE BEHIND THEM COMING GENTLEMAN. Ho, by the way, I tell you! Give me leave to remark that we also should be delighted to play now and again in a while, if you have not come to live here and will consider us. Be so kind, I say! Come along there, do!

LORD SMITH. I cannot brook these awkward noises which arrive in time to confuse me in mid-stroke.

VISCOUNT BROWN. Do not mind him. He is being sarcaustic. He is making game and thinks to be humoresque.

LORD ROBINSON. Oh no, my good chap, if I may say so, listen: It is because he is *not* making game that he is annoyed. Ho! Ho! Ho! Ho!

LORD SMITH. There! At last I am on the right lawn all correct. I now take the patter.

[*Each inserts his own ball into the hole.*

VISCOUNT BROWN. (*To the Behind Them Coming Gentleman.*) There, Sir, the hole is now disengaged. Play on, do, I beseech you, but kindly remember not to behave as if you were one of the not the Best People!

A-Boating

First class boatsmanship is a feather in the hat if it can be done but row-boat racing is done only by the younger sets, chiefly at Oxford-and-Cambridge. Now it may well occur that you be invited to Oxford-and-Cambridge to view the descendants of the Best People afloat. Good for you if you can show some knowledge of what happens, eh?

Boating Combats. Specimen englisch Epistle Recountant of the Eight-By-Eight Water Racing At Oxford-and-Cambridge.

Dear My Cousin Alice, Countess Williamson,

What ho? This I say by way of greeting, because of being so jolli here in Oxford-and-Cambridge during the seven days of marine struggles. All is cheeri and I am gay too.

In case you are she who is not familia with that which goes on along the streams, I will announce the things which take place. You see, I tell you, it is a question of striving, some a-gainst some, on board. In each schip there are eight who assist in moving her about by dint of waving their oarpieces, while one takes his place in the steerage and pulls the strings as cunningly as maybe. He is entitled the coxswain and is the one over the eight, for it is up to this one to scream advice when necessitous. Have you got me, eh?

Well then, I say, the fleet does not proceed side by side, for that would never do, because the torrent is slender. O no, by Jove! They cruise along indianwise, all between eachother, beginning at times various, according to the reputation they have gained at former regattals. Perhap you are she who

24

perks up her ear and demands how then can the one give the other the go-by and come in previous at the winning- sign? Well, I tell you, it is not controlled in such a faschion, I should think not!

Instead of flasching by in fine style, as many would like to do, I'll be bound, the scheme is that if one schip is more agile than she in front, the steersperson directs the nose so that it bangs the predecessor o such a wallop! Whereupon, the latter is unpossessed of her prior place and very nice too. What fun! In the next combat, she who bangs begins where she who was in front began before. Simple, eh?

What excitements indeed are given rise to by these activities! The partisans of crew after crew chog along the toepath, each a-schouting and dis-charging pistoles which, although chok-a-blok with leadless munitions, nevertheless are quite potent enough for my liking in the way of ejecting ever such big noises in order to urge on the navigators. Sometimes a joyous onlooker, who approves of the

triumph of a schip, will go all a-splasch into the water itself and become submerged in full dress until the immersion becomes too much for him and he relinquisches the stream, still gay in spite of such a wetting indeed!

Ho Ho! It is so fonni, you know! The maidens deck themselves in their biggest and best and saunter along, looking oh my what pretti pictures! And many students, who are not on deck helping their schip to carry on, follow about the maidens with the idea of cutting a dasch. But do you think the girl-people care a whittle for these? My aunt, o no! They are thinking all the time of the actual participators, who are the heroes of the day and have the blues, though not all those who are manning the schips have the blues, for a blue is only bestowed to the most skilful of all. Nevertheless to be a waterman of any sort is the correct passport to the affections of the fair ones and they who are not, but merely escort the girls arm-for-arm and spruce themselves tidily and consider themselves swells no end, find that a participator soon carries off the dearly beloved. Ho Ho! Very comic.

Next year, you must be among those present and see for yourself, eh?

Your obedient cousin and servingman,

VISCOUNT THOMPSON

Horsemanliness

Horse knowledgeabiliti (and lov) is scarceli not less than compulsory in englisch society so it is safe always to stress your horsemanliness and to vociferate how much you approve of the good beasts. Be warned that it may also be necessary actually to take a seat on one and stay there while it goes from one place to another which, unless it is in any case one of your habits, needs practice to avoid a state of topsiturvi.

The accurate noises are these:

Get along there, do! (*For commencing*)
Gee! (*For going on*)
Woe! (*For not going on*)

Typical Conversation at the Horseflesch-Market

LORD SMITH. I would buy a nag.

THE VENDOR. Certainly, milord. I have horses of all colours, of all sizes and of all shapes for dirty track-racing, hacking, leaping or the fox-chase. Examine, pray, the yellow dun!

VISCOUNT BROWN. Make it go at a footpace, in trot, in galop, and with loose rains.

LORD ROBINSON. It is a good ambler, by Jove!

LORD SMITH. It takes frights. It walks rudely. It jolts.

VISCOUNT BROWN. It jumps both ways.

THE VENDOR. No, indeed, milord, what ho! It is the cat which jumps both ways altogether, according to our englisch folk proverb saying.

[*All shake their sides with tittering. It is a choke.*

LORD ROBINSON. Ho! Ho! Ho! I am so tikled! I am so tikled!

LORD SMITH. Perchance we shall purchace the nag, but first we shall examine the others, Great Scot!

[*They depart, talking shops.*

THE VENDOR. Aha! They talk shops. We Englisch are a nation of shoptalkers! Aha!

(*This, too, is also a choke as well. Englisch chokes are o! so peculiar. Students are advised to chortle, for it is polite.*)

The Chase: Hoicks!

STUDENTS!

It may be that you will go in for hiring a nag and galloping about after foxen and other vermin in the company of folk with a like intention. But this should not be indulged in without being familiar with the rules of behaviorism, which are strict among such.

Dress.—Breeches (a trowser which dwindles below the knees) and a hunting-jacket of red stoff. You must be booted.

Noise.—It is unnecessary to take a trumpet of your own, but it is essential that you should imitate the cries of your fellow aggressors. But do not startle the horseflesch, lest you get run away with and made aschamed.

29

Conduct.—You are certain to be looked at askance if you attempt to oustrip the hunting-dogs, however great your zeal. Allow them to lead the way, for they must go first in order to sniff out the route of the quarry. At the same time, do not lag behind, for you will be thought too timid to progress with the others and if you disparage the agility of your nag, it may not be believed you. Also, do not relinquisch your steed for the purpose of opening gates and walking through, but allow him to lift you over the top.

If you should come tumble-down, do not be grumpi, but resume and join in the fun with as much zest as beforehand. You will then be thought up to as ever such a good fellow, which is the whole scheme, you see.

Useful remarques.

What a jolly run for our money!

How I don't like foxen!

Over we go, boys!

Joicks!

[*Pronunciation: Huött ä dscholli rön forr aur mönni! Hau ei dohnt leik föchsen! Ohwerr ui go, beuss! Jeuks!*]

Beasts to Pursue

Foxen (ugh!), ottres, he-deer, and hares,* but one at a time, please!, and with different dogs.

*****Not** bunnirabbits, the dear things.

30

A Chest Party

LORD SMITH. This year, winter makes itself perceptible.

LORD ROBINSON. I would winter past.

VISCOUNT BROWN. It frostles. Last night it rimed. Let us rap us warmly up!

LORD SMITH. The river is chockblocked with pieces of ice. Freezing! Thick enough sufficiently to be bearing.

LORD ROBINSON. What about a skate? Can I get a pair of skate lent?

VISCOUNT BROWN. Nay. One feels well only by the stove or not at all. Let us therefor commence a sporty party at Chest.

LORD SMITH. Where is the Chest board? I challenge at Chest!

LORD ROBINSON. I shall strive against you. Shall you direct the white pieces? Very well, then, I select the blacks. You putsch first! On!

VISCOUNT BROWN. I shall adjudge the contest. Play fair! Do not act like not a gentleman with low-hand tricks and sly shoves!

[*Play commences.*

LORD SMITH. Finely putsched! You have intricated the game anew.

LORD ROBINSON. You mock.

LORD SMITH. It is chequ-mate. You have gained the party. I am incensed. I do violence to my feelings!

LORD ROBINSON. Don't violence to your feelings! It is only a game! I gained it! How happy I am! How delightful! Charming!

VISCOUNT BROWN. How pleasant are these games in the winter season, when one cannot sport about without!

A Rubbre

LORD SMITH. I have just learnt some contraction bridge. What about a rubbre, eh?

VISCOUNT BROWN. Not a bad idea, I will say! But a fourth must be party to the scheme.

LORD ROBINSON. Well, here is Earl Hopkins. He shall participate.

LORD SMITH. Holla, Earl Hopkins! What if you were to be one of us for a rubbre?

EARL HOPKINS. Charming! I should esteem it a dignity to take hand. I am ever so sly at the game. Forwards, commence! Slice the pack, each one, so that we shall tell who with whom shall take sides and who be first at deal.

LORD ROBINSON. There! Earl Hopkins strives with Lord Smith as assistant and I with Viscount Brown, who distributes.

LORD SMITH. Ei! I have a pretty show. Look out, my good chaps, I hanker after a Greater Slem!

VISCOUNT BROWN. But it is not your place to initiate. It is to me. Before I reveal what I wisch to say, I must distinguisch between the quik tricks and the dead.

EARL HOPKINS. Get busi! Be some more nimble about it, I say!

VISCOUNT BROWN. I choose the suite of spades and contract up to three.

EARL HOPKINS. Counter!

LORD ROBINSON. Re-counter!

LORD SMITH. My aunt! This will never do by any means. I declare gamebid in no-trumpfs.

VISCOUNT BROWN. Go along with you! How tire-some, really! I can say nothing at the moment but will await developments.

EARL HOPKINS. Six glubs!

LORD ROBINSON. Oh my! Fancy!

LORD SMITH. Greater Slem in glubs!

> [*All give this the go-by.*

LORD ROBINSON. I to initiate? I give the Knafe of Diamants.

> [*Lord Smith at once throws on the queen.*]

EARL HOPKINS. (*Iresomely.*) Ei! Of what do you think? You can do no such thing as this! You are the Dumbo!

LORD SMITH. Eh?

EARL HOPKINS. You are he who deposits his card on the table and takes part no more except pass a remarque such as 'Not having a few hearts, partner?', should I fail to follow the suite.

LORD SMITH. Goodness me! Some game indeed, where one is left in the cold and has no fun at all, while all the other three conduct the sport alone! I do not wisch to be Dumbo.

34

EARL HOPKINS. Do not turn crusti, milord. For your part you must be Dumbo. See to it!

LORD SMITH. Well, I suppose I must do the necessary! But had I known, then not I to have called Greater Slem in glubs.

Art

At certain times of the year it is the polici of those who are in the know as regards correct behaviourism to interrupt sporty chat and mention a few things now and again with regard to art. It is excellent work to display some arty connection in your famili tree and perhaps to dasch off a thing of your own. But do not go too far by half, do not dub yourself a highbrougher!

Conversation Piece

LORD SMITH. To-day I have been to places of an artistik persuasion. The Britisch Museum, the National Gallerie, the Viktoria-with-Albert, and the Tate-and-Lyle.

LORD ROBINSON. Indeed? How nice! My female cousin paints in watering colour and in pastil. That seescape is due to her.

VISCOUNT BROWN. My sister is able to model. She is skilful in plastik.

LORD SMITH. It has been heard told that your artistik aunt has been observed portraying on pavements for petty casch!

VISCOUNT BROWN. I must confess it has been brought to my eers. But only on the Best pavements!

LORD ROBINSON. Nevertheless, to my mind, I think she is a not a lady to paint so.

VISCOUNT BROWN. Alas no! Do me the favour to have done with speaking of her while I am in society. My father, mind, has been hanged in the Akademy.

LORD SMITH. It is so pleasant to talk of matters of art. Let us practise with the pensels. Here is an easle!

LORD ROBINSON. How I love the sporty englisch art!

VISCOUNT BROWN. Let us trace a nice horse, in perspektiv!

LORD SMITH. At galop, full speed ahead!

LORD ROBINSON. With some milord on top!

VISCOUNT BROWN. How we are kultured, all three, in our spare time! Pass the paint!

3.

Lov

Lov
(Ho! Ho!)

I am not going so far as to say that a student would care for an espousal with englisch society, but these two specimen letters on the subjekt of lov (ho! ho!) should be studied as they somewhat descripe what it is good for a man in highlife to go in for being and give some idea of the Best attitude to ladifolk.

In England, lov (ho! ho!) should always be referred to in an archi way with many a sly whink and chukle, as if it were queer.

Specimen English Epistle Containing an Honourable Suggestion of Wedding Blis to a Pretti Lady of Equivalent Station.

My Dear the Honourable Miss A—!

Allow me! It is, I tell you, with certain feelings of finding my heart in my boot that I essay to salute you, charming A—, in these strains of cordiality and loving gusto. I do not wisch to rusch about in places where angels are not fond of treading, but I am so impelled to do so by inward flames, that I cannot assist myself. Therefor, I pray, be nice about it!

Perhaps it has been swum into your ken by now that I entertain in your direction predilections more enthusiastik than those of only amicability alone. It has now fallen to my lot to state that so it is and no doubt. I do indeed! Oh my! I fancy you!

Truly, for donky years I have cherisched in my besom the proposal of one day perhap attaining a state of husband-and-wife together with you alone. Now it is out and I have declared. Receive it with mersy, I beg!

Do not, for goodness gracious sake, swallow this down the wrong way! Pardon me, do, if you find I have what an impertinence! It is so evident to me that I am by all means less than nothing as good enough for you. But I suspire to the heights of blis and dare have some hopes. Brievely, I lov.

It is on bended knee that I write at you now and supplicate that you might see your way to an espousal jointly with me. Can it be done? I would be so glad, I tell you, if you would only! I protest that should you have me at no price, I shall be a great deal dismal, so that life will be no more of some value to me, so lavischly am I tender about you. Ei ! Some anguisch for my part, if you shoulder me cold!

At this stage I realize that up it is to me to pass remarques about my qualifications to be your hubbi. (Only to think of it, dear the Honourable Miss A— is so delicious!) Foremost, in the first place, before anything, I will say this. I have some quantities of casch. Ample. Sufficing for both of us each. That would be so O.K.!

Now then, I am good about the house. I know what. Not I he who permits asch and such from his cigarro to tumble from aloft and splasch the carpeting. I am well up to the mark in not being oh such a nuisance! Then again I will not sit to table at eve and disgruntle concerning the disches you prepare. Perhap you are she who wonders whether I might not perchance slink in tardily, having kept it up until ever so late, in a state of not all there, what with an abundance of liquors within ? Dear me, oh no! I cannot see myself! I am one for carousals and high jinking, but only especially, to celebrate some jolly eventuality. And I never get so that I diz and buz and behave clumsy. Well, I ask you! Beleive me do!

But I must not tell you a great deal too much in so many words all together at once. Therfor I say some more that I am so amiable about you. Please agree to wedding blis!

Your obedient servingman,

LORD SMITH (*Rodney*)

[*Postscripture*] If you do not shortly riposte, I shall permit myself to pass some more remarques concerning myself in person.

Additionle Self-References for Courting a Pretti Lady of Equivalent Station Towards Wedding Blis.

My Dear the Honourable Miss A—,

Since you have not as yet riposted to my epistle deglaring what an affectionate view of you I take and wisching that you might go so far as to undertake a betrothal in my company, I now make myself the allowance of some more addressing you and revealing to you what kind of a sort I am, so that you shall think a second time before making of me a dismal one for life-long, by saying me nay.

Well, I am devoted to going often to the theatre, kinema, music hall, the boxing, the wresting and flamework displayals, and always sitting down in the most expensive places with plusch seats and every advantage de lux. Beyond any shade of doubt you would accompany me, should you feel partial to activities of such a nature. As for musical performances, I am always there first at the concert pitch, with positions contracted for very previously. O dear yes! You should partake of all the enchoyments you could long for, to your heart's contents. I am ever so adept at distributing a good time, I will say!

Naturally I am a good sport of course. I would

not you thought me a milksap. Gracious, by no means! When the hunting dogs set up a quarry and tongue is given and the fox leaps along with the idea of escaping us, I am foremost among his following. At bird a-schooting, I never fail to discharge my firearm in the best direction and bring down the feathered friend stone dead. Let me say that at horse-polo I am always he who gains and at cricket no-one can persuade me to desist from striking the ball out of bounds.

I hope you do not have notions that I would not be fond of dancing about. The truth is I am ever such a one for waltzing, tango, and trotting. Never would I trip upon your heels and dismay you, so light of feet I am. As for chambre-music, of course I only enchoy the best music and would listen to you handling the pianoforte all day without breathing a word.

Now, lovli the Honourable Miss A—, I shall only repeat that I am enormously tender on your behalf. I must tell you some things about your beauti. Do not flusch, I say! Here is one who thinks you more lovli to gaze upon than someone else, whoever she be. Alas! that I have not the gift of the gub and so cannot set down in both black and white exactly my sensations of approval, but allow me to be so bold and riski as to pass a remarque of this nature: in my eye, you are a dearling of a young lady. I do so hope I do not commit a presumption, what?

Please, I implore you not to gilt me! Consider what you are about! And if you shall be so nice as to join forces with me in a matrimonial junction, then it shall be I who shall be dasched overchoyed. Now I have said my say and it just remains to see which way the cat jumps out of the bag. Please do not take many days to select yes or no as a riposte, for I am all agogue to ascertain whether it shall be wedding blis or unrequite lov for my part.

Your obedient servingman,

RODNEY (*Lord Smith*)

[*Postscripture*]

I have houser on the country and shooting-bogs. (Students should notabene that this should be added as an afterthink, so as not to give the appearance of taking side and being too much of a swanker. That would never do!)

4.

Humoristics

Englisch Humoristics

In England it is gratifying to obtain a sense of humour, for then you are taken for a cholly decent lad and for your lot it is 'Hail, fellow!' and 'Fanci seeing you some more, well I never!' in a contented tone.

Englisch humoristics are a bit rum and request careful planning out beforehand. These are the typical brands:

(i). Slapp-stick, slapp-dasch, back-slapp, and hit and run. (In fact hearti boister, generally.)

Do have a care how you employ these ways for laugh-and-grow-fat. With the ladifolk, for an instance, never subscripe to hearti boister, whatever be your custom at home, as the dear things are apt to fall about in the rough-and-tumple and receive a mischief.

No, I tell you, this sort of behaviourism is all very well and very risible too, but it is only for the masculines and even then should be restricted to times when all are gay, such as after meat.

Only so is it allowable to give the englisch Best people a putsch or two and prank about generally.

(ii). Sarcasticismus, ironics, and witty talkiness

These are harder to do than boister but can be very mirthy. Exempulars:

A. For menfolk.

When one says 'Really, I am not myself to-day', then rapidly riposte somewhat of this model—'Well then, let me know who you are instead, will you?' or 'Gratulations dear old fellow, ho! ho!' Say it with chuckling, lest you put his back up. Should this happen, then add: 'I say, keep your hair in!'

B. For ladifolk.

It is unwise to apply talk of such a description to she-friends, but it may be used to strangers who annoy. Thus, when, in a crowd, a weighty dame overtreads you on the toes, say:

'Dear me, my good girl, although I now perceive that you have not yet learned to stand on your own feet, it would be nice if you would vacate my toepieces!'

In all cases, if it seems not clear whether they comprehend the nature of your remarques, disclose a resounding titter or giggle to get things going. Otherwise retain a grim outlook according to the more modest behaviourism, which the good englisch society so dotes on.

(iii). Pun-fun

A modicum of the Best People assert that they eschew punning and deem it a social solecismus. They vilify the author of such and cry 'O-pun the door' in a manner to indicate resentment and groan outwardly. So take care of yourself before putting forward a dictum couched in this style.

You may find, though, that along of the Very Best People that money can buy, it is more of a dasched good proposition altogether indeed, but even here deprecation is sometimes of necessity and it is wise to be slightly schamefaced.

'Really, I talk away in puns and twos, sixteen to the doxen' might be a good thing to aver after realeasing a remarque somewhat too far-flung, in an attempt to be excusable. Or: 'Pardon my remarques, they slip out all too glibly for me!'

Puns, of course, are chokes in which the two main words are resembular. Owing to the menacing attitude adopted towards them, it is valuable to learn a set of phrases. Thus it would never do to shout 'Ho! Ho! What a delicious pun, I think!' only to hear the Best People complaining.

These dictums are fairly safe to use:

'He has punned! Ghastly! Does he indeed take us for not-wits?' (To be said in a confidential sideways to someone else.)

'Did you make that pun with aforethought or was it just a terrible accident?' (Await the riposte before deciding whether to guffaw or to sneer in the teeth of the responsible.)

'Never mind, so did Shakespeare.' (This is a first-class thing to say as a consolation prize when all are stern. Also it is, of course, always popular to allude to the literature of the realm in which you are extant and Shakespeare will pass for nearly everything.)

On the whole it is the action of he who is slier than his fellows to give the whole sorri business a wide berth. If you try the little game on yourself, you shall undoubtedly place your step on the wrong corn altogether or let slip something impro-prietorial. English is oh! how an easy language to offend society in as innocently as just-tumbled snow. You chatter in all simple-mindedness and suddenly lo! what a blusching and hostilities and no one will be explanatory.

What a blusching and hostilities

[*Vokabular*]
He who puns—*punster (fem. punstress), pundit.*
In a manner of punning—*punningly, punfully.*
A pun which all repeat—*a current pun.*

Sorts of Fun

Limriks—verses concerning personalities, averring something pretti sarcasticistik.

Praktikal choke—laying a petti ambusch for some person, such as applestart bed.

Spoonerismus—not for nordic Students.

5.

Approval of Animals

'Love Me, Loveaduck!'
(Approval of Animals)

If you can, lov as many animals as possible and pat and tikle them, especialli pupdogues and putzikats, which are very popular in England, whatever they may do. Of course, however, some animals must be disrelisched.

Loved.	*Disrelisched.*
Dogues.	*Foxen.
Kats.	Rats and mise.
Horses.	Wheasels and stoats.
Kanaribirdlings.	Budgers.
Tamed bunnirabbits.	Snaken. }
Tamed rats and mise.	Beetlers.} of course.
Singsong birds.	Wesps. }

*especially, by Jove! Ugh!

Childer, too, are doted on. When you are in a house where there are childer, it is good to ask the parent what he intends to do with his descendants in a scholarly way and with regard to careerism.

In Park and Zoo

LORD SMITH. I have much pleasure in this brisque strol in the Park.

VISCOUNT BROWN. What is so nice of a real englisch Park is how citizens are allowed to take steps on the grass. That is indeed amenable, eh?

LORD ROBINSON. So. Yes.

LORD SMITH. Lo! There are urchins in recreation. They play at Rogby. They scram down. Play up, I say!

VISCOUNT BROWN. I am fond of perceiving the young gambling about in the sunshine. It is a reminder of Spring shortly.

60

LORD ROBINSON. Now we are arrived at the space for keeping live beasts in good preservation to be looked at. A menadgerie. Shall we pay each a schilling in full and stare at the collection?

VISCOUNT BROWN. Oh Yes! Do let us!

LORD SMITH. I interest myself no end in the zoological.

[*They pay over and pass through the turnkey.*

LORD ROBINSON. Over against us is the shed of apes. They prank about. Behold the Orangutan!

VISCOUNT BROWN. No, no, my friend, I pray, admit that you are rong! You are barking at the rong kettle of fisch, I tell you! That is a Chinpanzee. There is the certifikate.

LORD SMITH. Cast it a monkey-gnut. But it will not take it. Very well then, I have here a grape. That will be a luxury indeed for the quaint creature.

61

LORD ROBINSON. Look, I say, it snivels the gorgeous morsel to test whether it shall be bonafide or no.

VISCOUNT BROWN. Here on this side sits a mandrill.

LORD ROBINSON. Gracious me! How grotesque is its nozzle!

LORD SMITH. Indeed yes. All coloured very flaschily. It has a ferocious outlook. I say, what if such a one were to squeeze between and place us all in jeopardy? Oh!

VISCOUNT BROWN. Come! That is enough of apes for just at the moment. They are not altogether pleasing animals. Let us emerge.

LORD SMITH. Which are those noises? I am convinced that something horrible has been loosed and is laying waste.

LORD ROBINSON. Stupid! It is but the sealions blurting for their repast. We are now approaching their bath.

VISCOUNT BROWN. Oh my! Great Scot! Did you also see? The sealion plunged from the cliff and munched the fisch in middle air!

LORD SMITH. The natation of these beasts is liable to much praise. They plunge with grace and swim most lithely.

LORD ROBINSON. No wonder—note how they are slippery!

VISCOUNT BROWN. Come, we are pressed for time if we would fain see all the show. Let us look towards the penguings.

VISCOUNT BROWN. Now here is the shed of reptilia. Frogues and toads and great snakes. There are also allegators. Shall we look and see?

LORD SMITH. Will every such creature be firmly restrained, that we come to no bodily pain from sting and fang? I am nervous of creeper-crawlers.

LORD ROBINSON. Take heart! We shall not be attacked. It is prohibited.

[They view the inmates.

VISCOUNT BROWN. Only see! There is a serpent which moves. It must be new.

LORD ROBINSON. It bites the glass, thinking to wound us. Those stains must be the poison. Ugh!

LORD SMITH. You are right. That is the lethal stuff, which remains on the pane. Oh dear! What if it were to seep through and envenom us all? What then?

VISCOUNT BROWN. Let us now inspect another species.

[They step out.

LORD ROBINSON. It is patent from these noises that we are now in the shed of parots and loud birds.

LORD SMITH. Well then if we address ourselves to yonder fowl, perhaps it will adopt a humane voice and pass a remarque. Let us try!

VISCOUNT BROWN. Pretty Poll!

LORD ROBINSON. Good morning, I say!

LORD SMITH. I hope it has been instructed to say

Yonder Fowl

the right thing. You never know what sort may have been speaking with it.

VISCOUNT BROWN. It is not in voice to-day. Never matter. Oh come! These noises appal me. Let us pass out!

LORD ROBINSON. There! The lioness sports with her young.

LORD SMITH. Ho! Ho! The young kub munches his mother's tail!

VISCOUNT BROWN. She says him nay, but yet he bites on.

LORD ROBINSON. Now she has given him a sharp tap.

LORD SMITH. That is by way of saying 'See that you do not do it some more.'

LORD ROBINSON. The panthre in the next partition does not look so pleasant.

LORD SMITH. No indeed. I do wish it would not look at me like that. It is most disturbing. Oh!

VISCOUNT BROWN. I am reminded that it is almost the hour for a good squared meal. What about it?

LORD ROBINSON. Agreed. But first I would regard elephants.

LORD SMITH. Then let us make some haste.

Childer

LORD ROBINSON. Look, my good chaps, here are some of my childer, hes and shes. Milady Robinson will say that they are little dearlings, but I am not always of the same persuasion, for the lads are prone to leap about and make noises, while the smallest daughter whines for no causes. The more aged lad is not here. He overbicycled himself yester. He went too far by half and is strained.

VISCOUNT BROWN. The eyes of that one over there playing with the toy are at cross purposes.

LORD ROBINSON. Indeed. It is inherited from my good wife, who is so nice and is now unfortunately out, alas, I regret. She has gone to a face-lifter's.

LORD SMITH. The elder lad who is grasping the tail of the kitten, which squeaks, will soon be of age of attending school. For where is he intended?

Lord Robinson. We intend him for the Playing-Fields of Eton.

Lord Smith. And after that for Oxford-and-Cambridge, of course?

Lord Robinson. Of course, though I must confess that it will be not easy for me to make both ends of the candle meet. But we will manage, however, I say. He shall follow in father's footpads, as we say in our englisch phrase.

Lord Smith. Ho! Ho! Then allow me to say, if you please, if you don't mind, that if he follows your examples he will be on a blue goose chase. He will be off to the dogs in no time and nothing will become of him!

Lord Robinson. I am resenting these observations,

my good Sir. I am one who is ever prepared to enchoy a good choke with the Best people, but I cannot but feel that you say this with a nasty taste in the mouth. I beg leave to point out that your critique of my characteristiques and carreer is one which no gentleman would give himself leave to apply to another gentleman!

LORD SMITH. But, I say, do not take on! I did but make a bit of fun. Come, do not carry on so dismaly! Surely you are not he who resents banter from cronies and I was but banting you! We are friends, eh?

LORD ROBINSON. Very well. Think nothing of it.

VISCOUNT BROWN. For what profession are the lads meant?

LORD ROBINSON. They are both meant for the Army and Navy.

LORD SMITH AND VISCOUNT BROWN. (*Together.*) How nice!

6.

London

London. Typical Conversations
(i). A Walk in London

LORD SMITH. Here we are at Trafalgar Square, which commembers a contest all at sea, in which milord Nelson was he who gained.

VISCOUNT BROWN. It is said that Horatio remained on the bridge until a bullet arrived and did him for. There is a piece of verses about it all.

LORD ROBINSON. I know, yes. He is one of the most famous englisch heroics.

VISCOUNT BROWN. There is Nelson's Colon in the middle of the square.

LORD SMITH. How there are pigeons!

LORD ROBINSON. Let us go down to Westminster on footpace.

VISCOUNT BROWN. Oh my hat! Which is yonder peculiarity?

LORD SMITH. It is a pedestrianist beacon.

LORD ROBINSON. To what end?

VISCOUNT BROWN. To this, that it marks the studs between which the footpacer shall not be vulnerable. Without, he is vulnerable. It is therefore the wiser course to keep between.

LORD SMITH. Who chose to place the signs by?

LORD ROBINSON. Some department of government or other. I am ignorant of policies.

VISCOUNT BROWN. Ho! Ho! The Ministry of Agrikulture, I should say! Ho! Ho!

LORD SMITH. Ho! Ho!

LORD ROBINSON. Ho! Ho!

VISCOUNT BROWN. Let us essay the transition.

[They step off the kerber.

LORD SMITH. Ei! That was a narrow squeal! I nigh came a-tumple!

LORD ROBINSON. Never mind, I say, my good chap, we are now safely overcome.

[They reach the paving and step on it.

VISCOUNT BROWN. See! The houser of Parliament!

LORD SMITH. Majestic.

LORD ROBINSON. Prime! That must I say!

VISCOUNT BROWN. List! Large Ben boombs the hour.

LORD SMITH. It is a typically englisch scene. Charming!

(ii). In the Wexworks

LORD SMITH. We have paid up. Now we shall enjoy the fun.

VISCOUNT BROWN. I pay attention with interest to Wexworks. The effigies are so vivid.

LORD ROBINSON. Yes. For instance, keep an eye skinned on yonder polizeman, who stands just without. Shall he be wex formulated to a striking likelyness to a polizeman, or shall he be a polizeman similar in appearance to wex? It is difficult to tell.

LORD SMITH. Pop a question to him and see whether he makes a riposte to it. If he does, then he is not wex.

VISCOUNT BROWN. I know. I shall place this dollar on his palm and watch if he wink an eyelasch.

[The polizeman closes his fist and makes off.

VISCOUNT BROWN. Ei! There goes my dollar. I do call that not cheap at the price, I must say! What a take-in indeed! Oh my! I am now the poorer.

[The others laugh out loudly, they think it is comic.

LORD ROBINSON. Come now! There is here a
Chamber of Horrors. Let us once repair there
and see for ourselves the frightful sights, which
are arranged in rows to startle us.

[*They enter in.*

LORD SMITH. Ugh! Ghastly! These spectacles make
my hair sit up no end with affright.

VISCOUNT BROWN. I perspire fluently with feelings
of timidity.

LORD ROBINSON. For my part, I enjoy these sensa-
tional views. Perceive that grisly relict of bygone
days, when persons were twisted and screwed!

LORD SMITH. No, I shall stay here no later. Such an
atmosphere repels a man of sensibility.

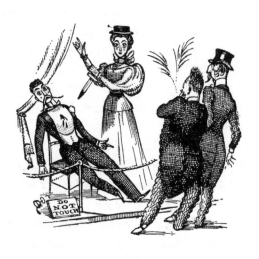

74

Viscount Brown. I am with you on your side.

Lord Robinson. Then I will see you subsequently in the room of calmer views. Historical sights and personages for example. So long till by and by! I shall remain and feast my eyes sumptuously.

[*They move on.*

Lord Smith. He is a man of not the same tastes entirely as our.

Viscount Brown. Come! Let us examine the other figures!

(iii). In the Kinema

Lord Smith. The young person who conducts us to our positions is dasched handsome. She looks very well.

Viscount Brown. She does indeed. But it was towards me and not towards you that she was looking. I glimpsed her just now.

Lord Smith. Dear me! You mistake my meaning quite. Or are you making some fun? You are a flippant fellow. You like to say the Rong Thing in countering my remarques. I was but commenting on the charm with which one is received in these Kinema palaces. All is magnificient.

[*They sit.*

Lord Robinson. I am so looking-forwards to this entertainment.

LORD SMITH. There is a comic englisch film, one hears.

VISCOUNT BROWN. Yes. But first there are the quaint mice, Mickey and Minny—a carton with accompaniment of noises. I dote on Mickey Mouse.

LORD SMITH. He runs about and makes us laugh. I too have soft spots in my heart also for the little fellow, although he is not britisch made.

LORD ROBINSON. There he is! Scrumptious!

VISCOUNT BROWN. Bravo Mickey!

A NEARBY SITTING PERSON. Beg Pardon, milords, but permit me to observe that unless you wish to cloy the enjoyment of others, it would be much nicer if you preserved total tranquilty up till the conclusion of the episode.

LORD SMITH. I see the fellow's point. I suppose he has the rights and rongs of it. Let us desist from passing remarks.

LORD ROBINSON. Agreed.

>   [*They keep peace until it is over.*

VISCOUNT BROWN. After this interval, there comes an exciting englisch film of brief duration before the big one.

LORD SMITH. It starts up.

LORD ROBINSON. Oh! The hero draws a pistole. Shall he pull the trigger and so dismay the villain? Or shall he withhold?

VISCOUNT BROWN. He has withheld. I would lief he had picked the rascal off and prevented the evil things he promises to do.

THE NEARBY SITTING PERSON. Milords, really!

VISCOUNT BROWN, LORD SMITH, and LORD ROBINSON. (*Together.*) Sch! Sch!

>   [*They say no more but gasp with excitement until the interlude.*

LORD SMITH. I am not so fond of these fellows who pound and stamp on the organ. It is too loud.

VISCOUNT BROWN. Never mind. The next film will be merry indeed. The chief roll is aped by one of the leading englisch comics.

LORD ROBINSON. I know him. He is a saucy man.

LORD SMITH. Indeed, I am all a-laugh already, by virtue of anticipation.

VISCOUNT BROWN. I too am prepared to hold my sides.

>   [*The film kicks off.*

Note—In England, films which hint at Not the Right Thing are marked 'A.1.' and childer must have a grownup alongside, to explain away.

(iv). Schopping

Lord Smith. In this schop are goods copiously supplied. One can verily purchace all and sundry that one is disposed to.

Lord Robinson (to a Vendor). Are you willing to show me linen?

Vendor. With much pleasure, milord. Of which quality?

Lord Robinson. Of the best. I will it for shirts.

[*He chooses the linen.*

Vendor. Shall I rap it for you, milord, or shall it be despatched to your place of residence?

Lord Robinson. Despatch it.

Viscount Brown. Now in this department one can procure jewellry, precious stone, and various knick-knacks. As for me I shall choose that beautiful diamant neck-chain for my good wife, the dear woman!, who remains at home. She dotes on diamant neck-chains.

Lord Smith. Have you cigarette cases in tortoise-skin and silvery tobacco-jars?

Vendor. Indeed milord, we have a wide assortment.

Lord Smith. Then I will return at a later time and choose and pick.

She dotes on diamant neck-chains

LORD ROBINSON. And this department is the one which deals in edibilities. Groceries and such. But examine that sugar. It is thick. It is not ground very mincely, indeed!

VISCOUNT BROWN. No matter, I require jam. Let the sugar pass—Show me pray some boxes of marmalade and jam of abricot.

[*He views the good things.*

How nice! Do three boxes of such for me up. Have a care, my good fellow! Ei! Rap it, I say, more gingerly or you will injure the fine jam.

LORD SMITH. Let us travel sky-high by the lift!

[*They enter the lift.*

LORD ROBINSON. How marvellous is science! One is here at one halt no sooner than one is there at the one higher. What a quickness!

VISCOUNT BROWN. We are now in the room of the small refreschments. What about some? I shall stand the treat. Tuck in!

LORD SMITH. I thank you so much. Indeed I could do with a small snick-snack. A bon, say, and a glass of stouter.

LORD ROBINSON. And I a sandwich and some ale.

VISCOUNT BROWN. How splendid it is being able to obtain everything in one establishment and partake in the meantime!

LORD ROBINSON. Yes, I am fatigued with buying. This ale makes me feel very refreshing. Here is to you!

(v). The Radio Box

LORD SMITH. I am for buying a wireless box. Will you also go along?

VISCOUNT BROWN. Certainly, it is very convenient to have the apparatus, so that one can plug up and listen to, at wisch. I do enchoy the Regional and the National and so on, etc.

LORD SMITH. It is marvellous what they can do. One overhears all sorts of informations at prodigious distances.

VISCOUNT BROWN. One can listen to the Empire and englisch entertainments.

[*They enter the radio place.*

LORD ROBINSON. That one looks proficient.

LORD SMITH. It is a bi-valve with a loud speaker.

VISCOUNT BROWN. I shall take a look-in, to see what is in the box.

LORD ROBINSON. Come now! One must not be a Noser-Parky. It is well to remember that 'Curiousness slew the putzi*'.

VISCOUNT BROWN. Goodness gracious! Do not be rude at me, I say, or I shall engage with you at fisticuffs and lay about me.

LORD SMITH. Lords! Lords! It is the privilege of a gentleman to quarrel how much he likes, but it would be meet not to bicker before the schop-person, who now approaches.

* Katze

SHOP-PERSON. Should I give you a practical demonstration of this box, milords?

VISCOUNT BROWN. Certainly, my good fellow go to it. Start it up.

[The box gives forth.

LORD SMITH. Oh, this is tikling my fancy! I have heard this man elsewhere—on the music halls.

LORD ROBINSON. I know him too. I have seen him perform conchuring tricks and feats of ledgerdemain. He conceals his traces most slyly. He is very dexter.

VISCOUNT BROWN. It is his comic back-answers which please me. Listen! Ho! Ho!

SHOP-PERSON. Shall I put it to yet another station?

VISCOUNT BROWN. Do. I am on tanterhooks to hear what shall follow.

[A talk makes itself heard.]

LORD SMITH. It is amazing how clearly one hears the fellow speak. It is a delightful box.

On tanterhooks to hear what shall follow

VISCOUNT BROWN. How interesting is this talk! Attend!

LORD ROBINSON. As for me, I have not really much love lost for such machines. I am more addicted to the pleasures of the table, preferring to bib wine in ample doses.

VISCOUNT BROWN. Almost you are not a gentleman!

(vi). In the Barber's

LORD SMITH. I will my heirs shall be snipped, trimmed, wasched, combed, and rinced.

BARBER. With pleasure, sir. Pray sit!

LORD SMITH. Shall you take a clean knapkin to me?

BARBER. Without doubt, sir.

> [*He schaves the milord.*

LORD SMITH. Oh what do you? You have cut my face. I am Lord Smith. I bleed.

BARBER. Oh milord! Woe! My aunt! But it is a nothing. I have but unsnipped a little pimpl!

> [*He attends to the heirs.*

LORD SMITH. Clumsy! You have scratched my eer with the comb. Oh! Comb me but softly! I will no curls!

BARBER. Do you require unguent?

LORD SMITH. Pray no. Brusch me a little and have done.

> [*He pays a little and hastes away.*

BARBER. (*Regarding the meagre sum.*) For my part, I
call that tip and run. Ho! Ho!

[*Englisch choke.*

7.

Countriside

Countriside

Specimen englisch Epistle to a Houser Agent of Inferior Station, Containing a Talli of Destrabilities in a Perhap to be Puchased House.

My Good Man,

Do not, I entreat you, be off with the idea that I am addressing you for purposes of entertainment and conversations. Far be this from the truth of the matter. You must understand that I am sending you this self-written epistle as a business proposition entirely. The fact is I intend to beget a mansion in which to store my family during the summer season and which would for my part be on tap for visits of a week-ending nature after the social here-we-go-round of the Wester End. Do you grasp my opinions, eh?

In the question of hugeness, the habitat must be comprehensive. At least do I insist on a dozen slumber apartitions together with scarcely less than a great many lounge-abouts and receptive chambres, each sufficiently voluminous to swing a cad in. So much for dimentions. In one compartment there must be all which is handi for billiarts, so that we can disport at pool and snook and entertain ourselves when kat and dog is being poured without.

Understand that I should not be he who should thrasch about with you the problem of draining and indoor saniti. Not I for such considerations, gracious indeed not! I will despatch some person, whose place it is to converse concerning such matters, and with him can you resolve a system.

As for the gardening spaces to circle round the mansion, I will say this. I require a great deal of full bloom, with red rose and white rose and all kinds of jacinth, daffydowndilly, and daisy-daisies among others included. You must see to this, I do insist. There must also be a plenty of turf and greens, with trees delicious to conduct a promenade under, so that townspersons shall come a-visiting and pass remarques such as: 'What a flaschi parade of rose-buds you have here, milord!' or, when they strol above the lawning, 'How I love your shady ways!'

I must have a golf-way placed fairly nigh, at which I can go round and round with my sticks and enchoy the sport and there must be a glubhouse where my good wife can be seated and sup alcoholics or pass round the time of the day with the other miladies until I should conclude the set.

Although I am he who is lord and master of automobiles galorum, I will that the mansion be so

nigh to the station that if one should take to casting stones, they would bounce among the trains, for I am on friendly terms with a handful of milords who prefer to eschew voyaging many miles in their own engines, lest the waggons be schocked or stained on the tough rostic pathways, so that should they be invited to be put up at my place, they would employ a train.

The house may be a longstanding affair, but with everything of the nicest inserted, such as elektric lamplight, central heat, gas in pipes, and many bath-places. There must be no dampness or cooling draughts, for I insist on being snog and cosi.

Kindly despatch now or never a talli of mansions of the nature of which I have been descriptive. And take care to depress the prices as much as can be. Do not, I warn you, have the face to do me in the eye and make me pay down the nose, with your tongue in your cheek, for I would not estomach it and will refuse to foot the bill, if you essay to unskin me on a bargain.

Yours Verily,

Lord Robinson

[*The ultimate paragraph is intended especially for the study of the most advanced students.*

Conversation Piece
A-Motoring

Lord Smith. This here is my limouzin. Leap in and we shall all be off, before you can say 'Lord Robinson.'

Lord Robinson. Ho! Ho! You make me a laughing-stick, my old boy. 'Jack Robinson' is what you should have said. Of course, I realize only too good-humorously that you are having a bit of fun, eh? I am one who can accept it with the right spirits. My heart is in the right-hand place. Therefore I am convolsed with a giggle. Ho! Ho!

Do not by any means have the idea that I am he who cannot tell what is in fun and what in deadli earnest. Ho! Ho! You comic, what!

VISCOUNT BROWN. However so many miles per one hour can the waggon go on at?

LORD SMITH. At threescore and ten.

LORD ROBINSON. Peace! You do not tell me! I never! What next, I wonder? What agility indeed!

LORD SMITH. To-day I myself in my person shall conduct.

VISCOUNT BROWN. Very well, set the conveyance a-going. We are prepared.

[*But something is not all well. The motor carriage proceeds hastily in a direction not intended.*

At threescore and ten

LORD ROBINSON. Ei! Ei! Gracious! You must have depressed the false button! Undo all this or we shall meet with an obstacle and collision something!

[*Lord Smith draws a lever.*

LORD SMITH. That is better. Now we are progressing in the direction towards which we were pointing, which is always securer, now isn't it?

VISCOUNT BROWN. Caution! The trafik lamp shows a yellow streak. Now it has struck pink. Come to a rest!

[*They evade the hazards and reach open Countriside.*

LORD ROBINSON. This is of the nicest. I am so enjoyable in this motorcar de lux. Some haste we bowl along with!

[*Upon a sudden, the auto crackles and still stands.*

LORD SMITH. Deary me! I fear a piston is not united any more!

LORD ROBINSON. Let us leave the schofeur to tinkle with the engine, while we stretch a leg.

[*They gain admition into a hotelry and call for jolly good ail.*

Specimen engliscb Epistle to an Aunt, Suggestive of Summer Plan.

Dear My Aunt,

First allow me to be solicitous and hope that you are in a rude healthiness, for I would not have it otherwise and would be a right gloomy one, if I sospected that you aled in any way and had diseases. Let me say that I hope that both you in person and my good uncle, Lord Biggs, are so fit as I am now, and also the young ones, on whom I dote, the dear little things!

I am in touch with you now in order to be suggestive about next summer holidays, as I have a plan for a jolli good time all round—either quite at sea (the South coastal) or somewhere rural all serene and tranquil and peacemeal.

I am, of course, as you know the proud possessor of several hundreds of tons of shipping—as waterfolk would put it—in the way of yachts, and I intend if possible to lead the life of an old seasalt, as the captain bold of one of my floating palaces, when the weather will be so good as to hotten somewhat more.

Now I am a-wondering whether you and my good uncle, Lord Biggs, and the childer too, would or would not like to put to sea with me, what about it, eh? If you hanker after life on the otion waves, as I hanker, and are not subject to indisposals when on board, riposte at once and we shall have ever such jinks, yo ho ho! If, however, you sospect the sea of being perilous and discomforting when the surface is not stable, we could adjourn to one of my rostic mansions and lead the lives of contri cousinfolk, miles away from some other place. The choice is to you. I must confess that for my part, I am for the saltwind and the seashore sand and the permanent waves of deep, dark blue. (Really! Even to envisualize life-on-board makes me quite poematic!)

Let me say that only the very Best people would be of the party. I should make sure to exklude any who might be thought to behave like not gentlemen or to hold disturbing views. Oh my, yes! Depend upon that! I am thinking of inviting from the Upper Chambre a wide selection of milords Spirituous and milords Temperance, who are accustomed to going into society and can act accordingly. If you accept, I tell you, your voyage companions shall be the best that money can buy, and who is he who can say fairer than that?

I am one of those—and I believe that you are of the same gidney—who consider that a summer voyage is of no real values unless one has a pretty hot time and can drench in the sunshine and become as brown in the skin as gnuts-in-May. I propose therefore to join the yacht at one of our most southerly ports, and, if the weather is not nice in the channle, to steer for a hotter place. You should, of

Only the very Best people

course, bring swimming attire and be prepared to enter into the spirit of the thing, for I hope to provide all sorts and conditions of jolliti and will arrange aquatic competitions in which even the most dignified persons may take part. What fun-and-games, eh?

I should be quite prepared to romp now and again with the childer, if you bring them along too, but do let me know how many you wisch to take, and I will have a special cabin upheld for them, where they can indulge in all manner of sportabouts and catch as catch can, and not be too tiresome. with their noises for us of a riper time of life.

I do hope that you will riposte immediately and agree to my kind offer.

Your obedient nephew,
Rupert, Viscount Jones.

Conversation Piece
In the Train

LORD SMITH. I say, it is fine. Let us go for a day on the country!

VISCOUNT BROWN. What a treat!

LORD ROBINSON. Yes. We shall take some trains and go out of London-town.

LORD SMITH. Ripping! What about Land's End?

VISCOUNT BROWN. Poof! Silly! That is too far, by half. Where is your geography? Really!

LORD ROBINSON. Very well. I propose the Downs.

VISCOUNT BROWN. Splendid indeed! On what railing are the Downs?

LORD SMITH. On the Southern Railing. Many trains ply between them and Victoria Station.

LORD ROBINSON. How much is a journey-card there in the first class?

VISCOUNT BROWN. Thither alone or to and fro?

LORD ROBINSON. To and fro. By nightfall must I be once more in the Wester End.

LORD SMITH. Come! Let us reck nought of the expense!

[*They proceed to the station in a taxi-kab and embark on a train.*

VISCOUNT BROWN. Pray take one of these cigarettes. They are very choice—rolled about by hand alone.

A STRANGE GENTLEMAN. I beg you for Heaven's

sake not to smoke here, sir. I regret to trammel your enjoyment, but I might turn unwell and incommodate the other voyagers.

VISCOUNT BROWN. (*Politely.*) Very well, sir. Granted I am sure! But allow me to draw it to your attention that there is a not-smoking partition in the last waggon.

[*The Ticketkontroloverseer puts in his appearance.*

TICKETKONTROLOVERSEER. Tickets please!

[*All show their cards.*

TICKETKONTROLOVERSEER. (*To the Stranger.*) Oh sir! You have a journey-card of insufficient value. This partition is a firster. Dear me! You must remedy this by some means, I tell you.

THE STRANGER. Allright, by George! I shall change my ticket for a rise in price. Also, kindly indicate for me a smokeless partition in the same class.

[*He betakes himself of.*

VISCOUNT BROWN. So! Now we can smoke away, willi-nilli. Take some!

[*They take cigarettes.*

LORD SMITH. Ei! I am not lit up. Strike fire! I thank you.

LORD ROBINSON. But see! The train draws to. And there are some Downs!

VISCOUNT BROWN. Loveli!

LORD SMITH. Beautiful!

LORD ROBINSON. How nice!

[*The train stands still and they climb down.*

8.

Anniversaries

Anniversaries

In England Christmas receives some attention indeed! and birthdays must not be allowed to pass along without notice and so I am inklusive of this conversation piece and this specimen epistle.

The Merry-Xmas

LORD SMITH. By and by Merry-Xmas shall be here, the season of depositing any amount of gew-gaw and fancy goods in the hosen of the childer.

VISCOUNT BROWN. Yes. I shall robe up by stealth as Santa Christmas and do the right thing by the little ones on Xmas Eve. Charming!

LORD ROBINSON. I am always so fond of Roast Turkisch and Plumb Pudding all a-flames.

VISCOUNT BROWN. My good wife is just presently buying sauce for the gander, which goes down so well as Xmas fare.

LORD SMITH. I say what! You shall all come on Xmas afternoon and quaff a dish of fine, French fizz with me. We shall make so merry!

LORD ROBINSON. Prime! Indeed we shall split a magnum of champagne wine. Oh good!

VISCOUNT BROWN. A magnum? Ho! Ho! A maximum!

LORD ROBINSON. Ho! Ho!

LORD SMITH. Ho! Ho!

LORD ROBINSON. How you are a comic! Such a one for the funny back-answer!

LORD SMITH. Listen, I pray, my good chaps, I tell you, it would be quite jolly after evening Xmas dinner to have the childer down for desert nuts and fruiting with candy-pieces and pulling crackles for the caps of paper to set at eachother,

in the good, old style of Merry-Xmas. Yes?

VISCOUNT BROWN. Scrumptious!

LORD ROBINSON. And we must also have the Xmas bush with silver tinsel and presents for all. I will see to that.

LORD SMITH. And play at Snapping-the-Dragon.

VISCOUNT BROWN. And Hunt-the-Slipper, in full cry.

LORD ROBINSON. And Consequentials, Up-Jenkers, Damb-Crambo, Scharaders, Rommy and all those. Oh yes!

LORD SMITH. What awful fun!

VISCOUNT BROWN. I am so looking-forwards to Merry-Xmas.

LORD ROBINSON. And I. I can hardly wait, but would lief begin now.

LORD SMITH. Do you intend to suspend your sock on Xmas Eve?

VISCOUNT BROWN. Absolutely. At Merry–Xmas, we are all still childer, no?

LORD SMITH. Just now we have been in the act of making the Merry-Xmas pudding. All the family took part in causing a stir in it, to bring good fortune.

VISCOUNT BROWN. Splendid! Did you also insert legal tender of silver and significant trinkets to be discovered inside the disch at Merry–Xmas?

LORD SMITH. Oh yes. The threepenny tit-bits and the Old Girl's Thumble and the Lucky Botton and all those. Fine!

LORD ROBINSON. So nice! We too have been making all ready; my good spouse has been busy with bunches of holly-busch. We have holly depending from every picture and ornament. It is beautiful, but one must look before one leaps, as there is prickle.

VISCOUNT BROWN. We have busches of mistletoe all over. How I enjoy the mistletoe ! At parties I take up my position below it and embrace all and sundry of those present, which are pretty girls, most heartily of all my good wife, whom I would not omit for anything.

LORD SMITH. Yes it is a popular englisch custom. But one must tread carefully. One must not overjump the limits of the good-taste. That would

never serve! Oh my, no!

LORD ROBINSON. Which presents are you giving?

VISCOUNT BROWN. I am buying my good wife a new fur coat, made entirely of minx-hide, rather costly.

LORD ROBINSON. My youngest is to receive a box of paints, so as to bring out an artistic temperance. It is splendid to give and receive at Merry-Xmas, is it not?

LORD SMITH. Yes, but especially to be he who is in receipt. Ho! Ho!

LORD ROBINSON. Three raising cheers, I say, for Merry-Xmas!

ALL. Hic! Hic! Hooray!

Epistle of Birthday-Anniversari Gratulation to an Old Chum-fellow of Equivalent Station, Comprising Therewith Sagacious Comment on Natalities in General.

Dear Milord Rupert, Duke Perkins,

I am sensible of abundant rapture as I lift up my pen, my dear old palcomrade, to address to you the felicitations which are due. I feel merry indeed to gratulate you by this upon the age of which you have just come—five and thirty years are you now ripe, is it not so? Well, to get down to no more ado about nothing, I will phrase myself in the usual manner: 'Several Happi Retorns of this Day!'

Suffer me to add in a more famili way that I am so delighted that you have reached this stage and no harm done. I hope you have many second helpings of the occasion and carry on, year in year out, day and night without stint, until you be at least a septuagesimarian or even over the eighty. And I also. Amen!

Birthdays, do you know, do not turn up but one time in every anno domino and, I say, we persons who know a thing or two should make the best of them while they are with us. Allow me to explain that people are of the minds in this matter. There are those who are fond of being in a birthday each annual time such a thing occurs, and there are those who deny the agreeability thereof, saying 'Oh dear no! Not for me, I tell you, I am not he who uses birthdays. I have no lust to be put in remind of each stage of life-on-this-world. Of birthdays I take the dismal view. Do not, therefore, I beg, be so displeasant as to gratulate me upon such a to-do'.

Now I am by no means he who casts in his choice with those who desist from recognizing these occasions when they see one. Pon my word, I should think not indeed! I will be prepared to allow that each and every natality is indeed a milestone along the voyage towards our ultimate reposals, but what I am fond of saying is that there is no help for it but to schrog the eyebrows and receive the inevitable with quietude and resignment. I am oft inquiring what the Duce can one do about it, eh? And the riposte is 'Absoluteli knix'. Exhibit to me, if you please, I beg your indulgence, him who glaims to be in a position to take the hand of time by the forelock and halt it! The head of such a one would be too big for his boots. He would be somewhat of a self-recommender, that chap! It would be wise to pinch the salt while listening to him.

Can the Ethiopiate unwrap himself and exchange his skin for better or for worse? Gracious, not at all! If the leopard cat should feel not at home among his spots, is he able to say: 'Not to-day, I tell you, give me some of better quality?' Whew! What notions!

As much out of the question, if not further, is it to essay to persuade nature to desist from taking its course. Wherefore growse at the pangs of seniliti? To what good resultant? To none. Therefore I say munch, sup, be merry and jubilious! Stuff the flowing bowl with wines and song and mark your natal occasion with music and blis! Lead a pretty dance indeed! Unbend yourself! Discork the bubbli and bid the best people admire the taste! Go so far as to return home in the company of the milkperson! Do quantities of dancing about with the ladyfolk and salute them copiously when they gratulate you! That is how to use a birthday, believe me! Try it on!

Now I am aware that there is a habit of backing

Quantities of dancing about

108

gratulations up with some good thing by way of presentment. So I bid you recite to me the name of that which kiddles your fancy and I shall constrain myself to make a point of taking possession of it, for love or money, and despatching it to you at the double. It shall be, I promise you, whatever it is, the best, at the price, that money can buy!

Your obedient servingman,

PERCY (Viscount Brown)

Noted Festivals

Merry-xmas, newyear, bank-on-holiday, Hallo! Een, gunpowder plan day, 12th night, foolday, birth-days and anniversaries of wedding-blis.

Two Epistles for
Idiomatic Study

Sommonsed! An Espistle to the Magisters, Detailing the Wherefore of the Trespass, in Riposte to a Sommons.

I

Honourable Worshipfuls,

I have this morning been in receipt of a good sommonsing from the arms of the law as a resultant of a slender accidental, which had being on or about some days ago, while I was being moved along by my schofeur in my motor vehicular. I consider it judicious to correspond with you so that you may apprehend the facts of the occurrence from my own lip. I have also a few slurs to cast at the konstabular in command of the affair. He should be blown up and ticked off, I tell you, for giving me what sauce indeed! A sound tap close to the knukle would take that chap a peg down!

The accidental came off allright—I do not say that nay. Let me expose how it has befallen. The machine was scrambling along at a good round velociti, for I had been bidden into society and was somewhat behind the time. Well, I bechanced to throw my gaze through the window and there, whom did I eye but a ever such a nice girl, a blondaine of the variety I particularly appreciate. My heart went pat-a-cake to see her, so well decorated was she with pretti features and so trimly habited in a plouse which became her supremely. You yourselves would have been all a-stare, I warrant. (I hope you will not think I take a freedom to say this?)

Now I am not one of these milords who disdain their schofeurs and prefer not to address them, except in requiring a destination, so I tug the schofeur among his ribs, whinking knowledgeabli at him, and said: 'How handsome is the damsel!' Well, he served himself with a view of her and the next instanter a lampstick desisted us!

At once I quitted the vehicular and closely eyed the lampstick, which I perceived was not too much injured, but only a little renched. I was about to resume the limouzin, when the konstabular marched up and clenched me, as if I had been a

My heart went pat-a-cake

114

felon of the deepest water! Oh my! I decried him volubly and bid him ungrasp me.

Then, seeing that I was in haste and that the lampstick was easily curable, and considering my station, I proposed to him that nothing should be said about the accidental. 'Let the whole affair remain a secret between you, me, and the lamp-stick!' I said. (Ho! Ho!)

The konstabular burst out into a chain of regretful things to say and even when I told him who I was, he refused to keep them to himself but continued to describe me. I looked at him askance, gave him my card and the name of the schofeur and gave orders that I should be taken away. It is of such cheeki behaviourism that I grumple.

The summons is, of course, naturally addressed to the schofeur in person and I do not intend to see the inside of a police court, you may be sure! I must consider my place.

But I have deep feelings about the affair and now that I have related to you the just cause of the whole to-do, I hope you will do the right thing and permit the schofeur to go scot free without a stain. You may tax me with the collapse of the lampstick, when it comes to financing the restoration, I will gladly fork it up.

As for the konstabular, he must be made to com-prehend that he shall not mouth impolitenesses like that, especially to milords. Kindly inflict a significant chastisement and command him to beg my pardon in both black and white. Then perhaps I will oversee the whole matter and say no more on the subject.

Your obedient servingman,
VISCOUNT BROWN

II

Lible! An Epistle to the Author of Skandle-manger Notes, an Acquainted of Equivalent Station, in a Press Sheet

Dear Milord Thompson,

Bless me! I am oh dear so grievous! It is what I do not care very much for doing, to rejoinder to the remarques of your very own which have been made public property in the news, for which you put pen to paper, but alas I am compelled to registre a murmur against certain of these which put me out and make me look oh what a silly fellow!

You and I must come to gripes and affect some sort of an understandment, for you see, although the things which you infer against me may be nothing-but-the-truth, yet it is not the act of he who is a gentleman to put them at the disposal of all who read. It is the jolly limit, really! I say!

Now I am well aware that once-on-a-time, I was a bit of a someone, who went in for making whoopi and generally burning the candles at their ends, and I was not for hiding the light below a buschle, for I was all a-boast at my ragging and raising the devil very.

But what you must sit up and take notice about is that all that is now bygones-be-bygones and I have now become a man about and someone to be looked up towards, so that if I should go so far as to merry-make and carry on, it is not to be schrieked from the houseroofs but to be kept under lock and key and nobody the wiser, please understand.

What you penned concerning me being arrested in a dance klub and being unkind to a konstabular, only to be deprived the next morn of a guinea or more by the magisters' bunch, is of course quite so and just my style, but it does not do for a person of my station and seniliti to blemisch my character in such a way and it is about time that you comprehended that discretion gives better value.

I shall be glad to have your apologi by postal comeback. Your humble servingman,

DUKE EDWARDS